The Evolution of Modern Data Architecture

Dipankar Mohanty

ISBN: 978-1-972004-42-5

Dedication

This book is lovingly dedicated to my mother, who left us on October 21, 2024. Her strength, wisdom, and unwavering belief in me have been the foundation of everything I pursue. *The Evolution of Modern Data Architecture* is not just a reflection of ideas and progress, but also a tribute to the values she instilled in me: perseverance, curiosity, and integrity. Though she is no longer physically present, her guidance continues to inspire every page of this journey. This work stands as a small token of gratitude and remembrance for her endless love.

Acknowledgments

This book was written with a simple goal: to bring clarity to the rapidly evolving world of modern data architecture. As organizations continue to navigate growing data complexity, cloud transformation, analytics, and artificial intelligence, I felt the need for a practical and structured perspective that connects foundational concepts with real-world architectural thinking.

I am deeply grateful to the global community of engineers, architects, researchers, and technology practitioners whose ideas and innovations continue to shape the future of data systems. Their work has influenced many of the concepts explored throughout this book.

I would also like to thank the organizations and teams that continue to solve difficult data challenges every day. The realities of fragmented systems, scalability concerns, governance requirements, and AI adoption inspired many of the discussions presented in these chapters.

Most importantly, this book is rooted in values that extend beyond technology: curiosity, perseverance, learning, and integrity. Those values guided this work from the first page to the last.

I hope this book helps readers not only understand modern data architectures, but also appreciate the important role they play in building intelligent and future-ready organizations.

— *Dipankar Mohanty*

Introduction

Over the past decade, data has become one of the most valuable assets for organizations across every industry. Businesses today collect information from countless sources, including applications, transactions, devices, customer interactions, sensors, and digital platforms, in different formats. This explosion of data has created enormous opportunities for organizations to gain insights, improve decision-making, and build intelligent products powered by analytics and artificial intelligence.

Data volume is increasing exponentially, and the challenge of managing it has grown accordingly. Many organizations continue to face challenges due to fragmented systems, siloed data pipelines, and duplicate datasets, leading to inconsistencies across their data landscape. Different teams often build their own solutions, leading to data silos that make it difficult to create a unified and trustworthy view of information. As a result, poorly designed data environments often slow organizations rather than accelerating innovation.

At the core of this challenge lies a fundamental issue: data architecture. The way data is collected, stored, processed, governed, and delivered ultimately determines whether an organization can truly become data-driven. Yet, the rapid pace of technological evolution has made the landscape of data architecture increasingly complex and often difficult to navigate.

Today, professionals encounter a wide range of architectural paradigms, including data warehouses, data lakes, lakehouses, data mesh, and data fabric. At the same time, an expanding ecosystem of platforms and tools promises to simplify data management. While these innovations offer powerful capabilities, they also introduce a new problem by further complicating how these components fit together into a coherent and sustainable architecture.

For many teams, the challenge is not a lack of technology, but a lack of clarity. Leaders and engineers are often forced to make architectural decisions while navigating conflicting opinions, vendor claims, and rapidly changing trends. Without a clear framework for understanding modern data architectures, organizations risk building overly complex systems that are difficult to scale, govern, or adapt to future needs.

This book, The Evolution of Modern Data Architecture, is designed to simplify the complex landscape of modern data architecture and provide practical guidance for building scalable and reliable data platforms. It explores the evolution of data architectures, from traditional warehouses to modern lakehouses, streaming systems, and AI-ready platforms, while explaining the core building blocks that power today's data ecosystems. Rather than focusing on specific tools or vendors, the book emphasizes architectural principles, design patterns, and decision frameworks to help readers understand and select the right data architecture to achieve their organizational goals.

Contents

Dedication v

Acknowledgments vii

Introduction ix

Chapter 1: The Evolution of Data Architectures 1

Chapter 2: The Core Building Blocks of Data 17

Chapter 3: Understanding Modern Data Architecture 28

Chapter 4: Choosing the Right Architecture for Your 39

Chapter 5: The Modern Data Platform Blueprint 48

Chapter 6: Eliminating Data Silos and Pipeline 58

Chapter 7: Designing AI-Ready Data Architectures 68

Chapter 8: Real-World Data Architecture Patterns 78

Conclusion 88

Chapter 1: The Evolution of Data Architectures

Data architecture did not emerge overnight. The systems used by organizations today are the result of decades of technological evolution. As businesses generated more data and demanded deeper insights, data architectures evolved to support growing volumes, new data types, and advanced analytics capabilities.

Understanding this evolution is important because modern architectures, such as lakehouses and AI-ready data platforms, are built on lessons learned from earlier systems. This chapter traces the journey from early Database Management Systems (DBMS) to modern lakehouse architectures, highlighting the strengths and limitations of each stage.

1.1 Early Data Management Systems

In the early days of computing, data management was relatively simple because the volume of data was small and the number of users accessing the data was limited. Most organizations stored information in basic file systems where applications directly managed their own datasets.

The earliest digital data systems relied on Database Management Systems (DBMS). These systems were designed primarily to support transactional operations, such as banking transactions, inventory updates, and order processing.

The most widely adopted model was the relational database model, introduced by Edgar F. Codd in the 1970s. Relational databases organize data into structured tables consisting of rows and columns. These tables can be queried using structured query languages such as SQL.

Common enterprise DBMS platforms include:

- Oracle Database
- IBM Db2
- Microsoft SQL Server
- MySQL

Early Database Architecture

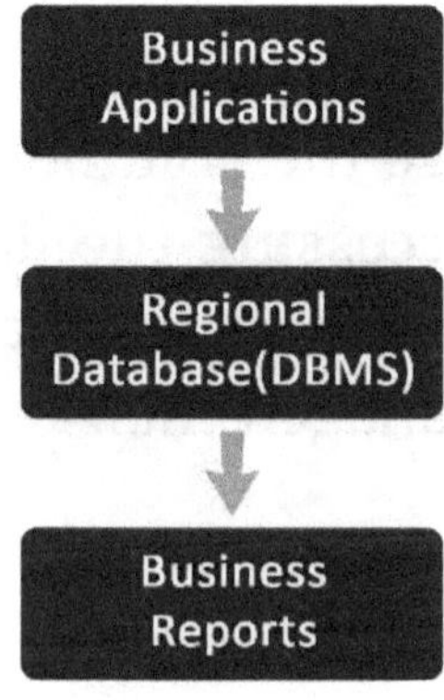

These systems were highly reliable and optimized for Online Transaction Processing (OLTP) workloads, as they ensured fast, consistent, and accurate handling of large numbers of small, concurrent transactions while maintaining data integrity through strict consistency and normalization.

Advantages

- **Strong data consistency and integrity** – Ensures accurate and reliable data using constraints (e.g., a bank transaction won't allow invalid account balances).
- **Efficient handling of transactional operations** – Optimized for frequent insert, update, and delete operations (e.g., processing thousands of daily orders in an e-commerce system).
- **Mature ecosystem and standardized query language** – Uses widely adopted SQL with strong community and tool support (e.g., easy integration with reporting tools).
- **Reliable backup and recovery mechanisms** – Provides robust methods to restore data in case of failure (e.g., recovering a database after a system crash with minimal data loss).

Limitations

- Limited scalability for extremely large datasets
- Difficult to store unstructured data such as logs, images, or videos
- Expensive infrastructure for large-scale analytics

- Not optimized for complex analytical queries

[Note: As organizations began generating and storing larger volumes of data, the limitations of transactional systems became increasingly evident. They needed platforms specifically designed for analytical processing rather than day-to-day operations. This need led to the emergence of a new paradigm in the data world, the data warehouse.]

1.2 The Rise of Data Warehouses

During the 1980s and 1990s, organizations began adopting relational database systems that allowed structured data to be stored in tables and accessed through standardized query languages such as SQL. These systems improved data consistency and enabled better reporting capabilities.

However, operational databases were designed primarily for transactional workloads such as order processing, customer management, and financial transactions. Running analytical queries on these systems often slowed down operational applications.

To solve this problem, the concept of the data warehouse was introduced.

A data warehouse is a centralized repository designed to store historical data from multiple systems in a structured format optimized for analytical queries.

The concept of the modern data warehouse was popularized by Bill Inmon and Ralph Kimball.

Data warehouses introduced several important innovations:

- Integration of data from multiple operational systems
- Structured schemas designed for analytical queries
- Historical data storage for trend analysis
- Separation of transactional and analytical workloads

Organizations used ETL pipelines (Extract, Transform, Load) to collect data from operational systems and load it into the warehouse.

Typical data warehouse platforms include:

- Teradata
- Snowflake
- Amazon Redshift
- Google BigQuery

Advantages

- **Optimized for analytical queries** – Designed for complex queries on large datasets (e.g., generating sales trends over several years).
- **Centralized business metrics and reporting** – Provides a single source of truth for key metrics (e.g., consistent revenue figures across all dashboards).

- **High performance for structured analytics workloads** – Efficiently processes structured data for fast insights (e.g., running aggregations on millions of records).
- **Strong governance and data modeling capabilities** – Ensures well-defined data structures and access control (e.g., role-based access to sensitive financial data).As digital platforms expanded, organizations began generating massive volumes of semi-structured and unstructured data, which traditional data warehouses struggled to handle.

Data Warehouse Architecture

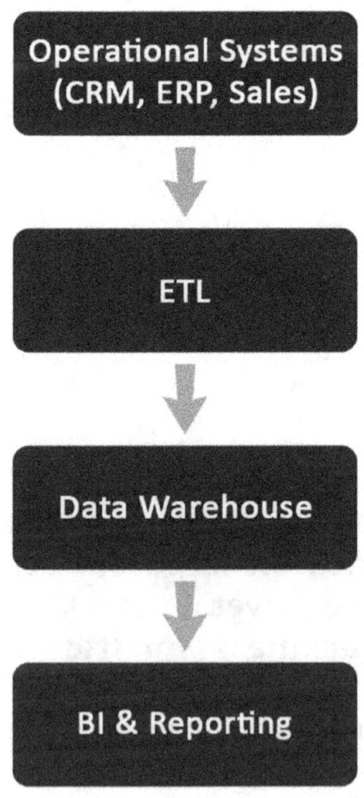

Limitations

- Designed primarily for structured data
- Expensive to scale for very large datasets
- Slow ingestion for rapidly growing data sources
- Limited support for advanced analytics and machine learning

[Note: However, traditional Data Warehouse (DWH) systems had several inherent limitations. They were primarily designed to handle structured, relational data and relied heavily on predefined schemas. As data volumes grew, scaling DWH platforms often required expensive infrastructure upgrades and complex performance tuning. Additionally, these systems struggled to efficiently process semi-structured and unstructured data such as logs, images, and streaming data. As organizations began generating diverse and massive datasets, the limitations of traditional DWH systems became more apparent, creating the need for more flexible and scalable data architectures.]

1.3 The Emergence of Data Lakes

In the early 2010s, organizations began collecting massive volumes of information from web applications, mobile devices, sensors, social media platforms, and machine-generated logs. Much of this data was semi-structured or unstructured, making it difficult to handle in data warehouses as well as in traditional relational systems. As a result, organizations began adopting data lakes to address the limitations of data warehouses and relational DBMS.

A data lake is a large-scale storage system that enables organizations to store structured, semi-structured, and unstructured data in its raw form. Moreover, it allows data to be retained in its native format, providing flexibility for diverse analytical and processing needs.

Data lakes allowed organizations to collect and store diverse data types, including:

- Log files
- Sensor data
- Social media content
- Images and videos
- IoT data streams

Unlike data warehouses, which require predefined schemas, data lakes use a schema-on-read approach. This means the data structure is applied only when the data is analyzed.

Advantages

- **Extremely scalable storage** – Can handle massive volumes of data by scaling horizontally (e.g., storing petabytes of log or sensor data).
- **Supports structured and unstructured data** – Accommodates diverse data types in a single repository (e.g., combining tables, text files, and images).

- **Lower storage cost compared to traditional warehouses** – Uses cost-effective storage solutions like object storage (e.g., storing large datasets at a fraction of warehouse costs).
- **Enables advanced analytics and machine learning** – Provides a foundation for complex analysis and AI models (e.g., training recommendation systems on large datasets).

Data Lake Architecture

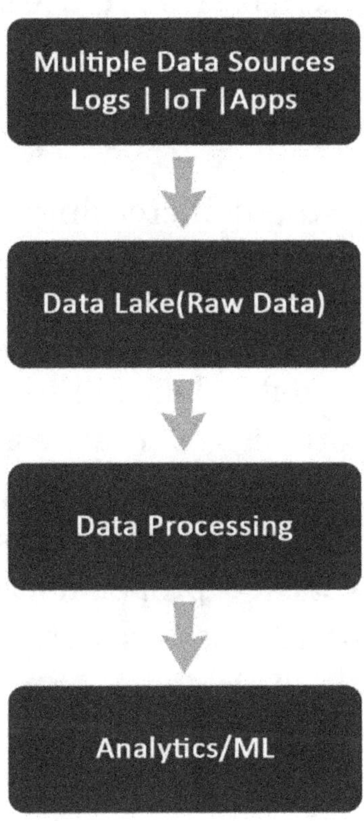

Limitations

- **Still an evolving architecture with emerging standards** – Tools and best practices are still developing, which can lead to inconsistencies (e.g., different platforms may implement features differently).
- **Requires strong metadata and governance frameworks** – Effective management of data definitions and access is essential to avoid confusion (e.g., without proper metadata, users may not understand dataset meanings).
- **Some workloads may still require specialized systems** – Not all use cases perform best on a lakehouse (e.g., real-time streaming or highly complex transactional systems may need dedicated solutions).

As organizations stored increasing amounts of data in lakes, they faced challenges in managing data quality, metadata, and analytics performance.

[Note: However, data lakes introduced their own challenges. Without proper governance and structure, many data lakes gradually turned into what practitioners called "data swamps." These environments contained large volumes of data but lacked proper documentation, quality controls, and governance. As a result, finding trustworthy data became difficult. This led to the next stage in the evolution of data architectures.]

1.4 The Lakehouse Architecture

To overcome the limitations of both data warehouses and data lakes, a new architecture emerged: the lakehouse.

The lakehouse architecture combines the scalability of data lakes with the data management capabilities of data warehouses.

Technologies such as the Databricks Lakehouse Platform and Delta Lake introduced features that bring warehouse-like capabilities to data lakes.

Key capabilities of lakehouse architectures include:

- **ACID transactions** – Ensure data operations are reliable by guaranteeing Atomicity, Consistency, Isolation, and Durability (e.g., a data update either fully completes or does not occur at all).
- **Data versioning** – Maintains historical versions of data, allowing users to track changes and roll back to previous states (e.g., restoring a dataset to an earlier version after an error).
- **Schema enforcement** – Ensures data follows a defined structure and format when written (e.g., preventing incorrect data types from being inserted into a table).
- **Unified analytics and machine learning support** – Enables both analytical queries and machine learning

workflows on the same data platform (e.g., using the same dataset for dashboards and predictive models).

In a lakehouse architecture, organizations store data in a central lake but apply governance, indexing, and metadata layers that make the data easier to query and manage.

Advantages

- **Unified platform for analytics and AI** – Allows both business intelligence and machine learning on the same system (e.g., using one dataset for reporting dashboards and predictive models).
- **Supports structured and unstructured data** – Handles diverse data types such as tables, logs, images, and videos (e.g., combining customer records with social media data).
- **Reduces data duplication across systems** – Minimizes the need to copy data between warehouses and lakes (e.g., avoiding multiple storage of the same dataset for different teams).
- **Scalable and cost-efficient storage** – Uses distributed storage that can grow as needed at lower cost (e.g., storing large volumes of data on cloud object storage).
- **Improved data governance compared to traditional lakes** – Provides better control, security, and data quality (e.g., enforcing access policies and tracking data usage).

Lakehouse Architecture

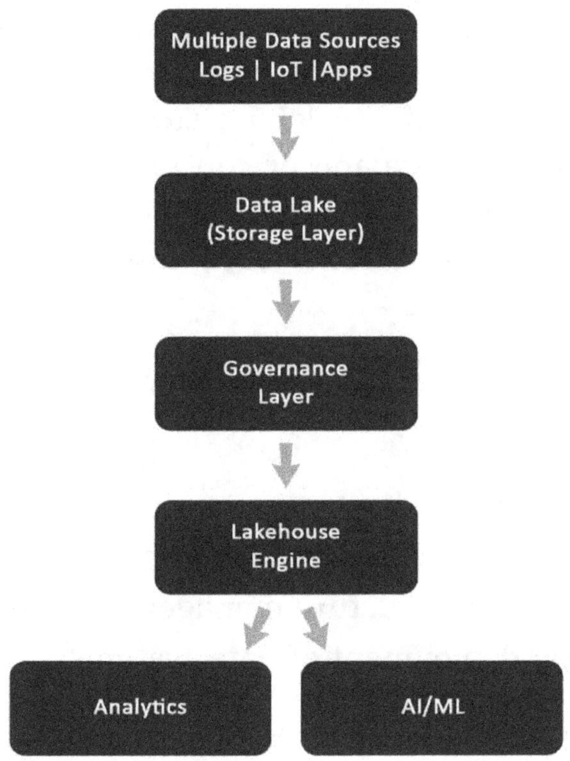

Limitations

- Still an evolving architecture with emerging standards
- Requires strong metadata and governance frameworks
- Some workloads may still require specialized systems

1.5 Cloud Computing and the Architecture Revolution

The emergence of cloud computing dramatically changed how data architectures are built and managed. Cloud platforms introduced scalable storage and compute resources that could expand or contract based on demand. Instead of investing in expensive on-premises infrastructure, organizations could now build flexible data platforms in the cloud.

Cloud-native data platforms brought several key advantages:

- Elastic scalability
- Separation of storage and compute
- Lower infrastructure management overhead
- Faster deployment of data systems

New platforms emerged that simplified analytics and data engineering workflows. These platforms allowed teams to process massive datasets without managing complex infrastructure.

Cloud computing also enabled the development of modern architectures that combine the strengths of both data warehouses and data lakes. One such approach is the lakehouse architecture.

1.6 Why Data Architectures Continue to Evolve

The evolution of data architectures is driven by several ongoing trends.

First, the volume of data continues to grow rapidly. Organizations are collecting information from an increasing number of sources, including IoT devices, digital platforms, and automated systems.

Second, analytics expectations have expanded. Businesses now require real-time insights, predictive analytics, and AI-driven decision-making.

Third, organizational structures are changing. Modern enterprises operate with distributed teams and domain-specific data ownership, which influences how data platforms must be designed.

Finally, artificial intelligence and machine learning are becoming core capabilities for many organizations. These technologies require scalable data infrastructures that can support experimentation, training, and production deployment of models.

As a result, data architectures must continue to evolve to meet these demands.

The key lesson from this history is that there is no single architecture that works for every organization or every use case. Instead, successful data architectures are built by understanding fundamental principles and adapting them to specific business needs.

In the next chapter, we will explore the core building blocks of data architecture. By breaking complex systems into simpler components, we can better understand how modern data platforms are designed and how different architectural patterns are constructed.

Chapter 2: The Core Building Blocks of Data Architecture

Modern data architectures may appear complex because they involve numerous technologies and tools. However, when viewed from a structural perspective, almost every data platform is built using a common set of foundational components. Understanding these components is essential for designing scalable, reliable, and maintainable data systems.

Rather than thinking about data architecture in terms of specific technologies, it is more useful to view it as a combination of core building blocks that work together to move data from its origin to the people and systems that consume it.

This chapter explores those building blocks and explains how they form the foundation of modern data platforms.

2.1 Data Sources and Data Generation

Every data architecture begins with data sources. These sources represent the origin points where data is created, captured, or generated.

In modern organizations, data is produced by a wide range of systems and activities. Some of the most common data sources include:

- Operational databases from business applications
- Customer relationship management (CRM) systems
- Enterprise resource planning (ERP) systems
- Mobile and web applications
- IoT devices and sensors
- Third-party APIs and external datasets
- Log files generated by applications and infrastructure

Each source produces data in different formats and at different speeds. Some systems generate highly structured transactional data, while others produce semi-structured or unstructured data such as logs, images, or text.

Because these sources are often distributed across multiple platforms, the first challenge in any data architecture is capturing and consolidating data from these systems efficiently.

2.2 Data Ingestion and Integration

Once data is generated, it must be ingested into the data platform. Data ingestion refers to the process of collecting data from source systems and moving it into a centralized storage or processing environment.

There are generally two main ingestion approaches:

Batch Ingestion

Batch ingestion moves data at scheduled intervals. For example, a system may extract data from operational databases every night and load it into an analytics environment.

Batch pipelines are commonly used for:

- Financial reporting
- Historical analysis
- Data warehousing workloads

Real-Time or Streaming Ingestion

Real-time ingestion captures data continuously as events occur. This approach enables systems to process and analyze data with minimal delay.

Streaming pipelines are commonly used for:

- Fraud detection
- Real-time analytics dashboards
- Monitoring and alerting systems

Data ingestion pipelines often perform basic tasks such as filtering, validating, or enriching incoming data before storing it in a data platform.

Data Ingestion Flow

This simple flow illustrates how raw data travels from operational systems into the storage layer of the architecture.

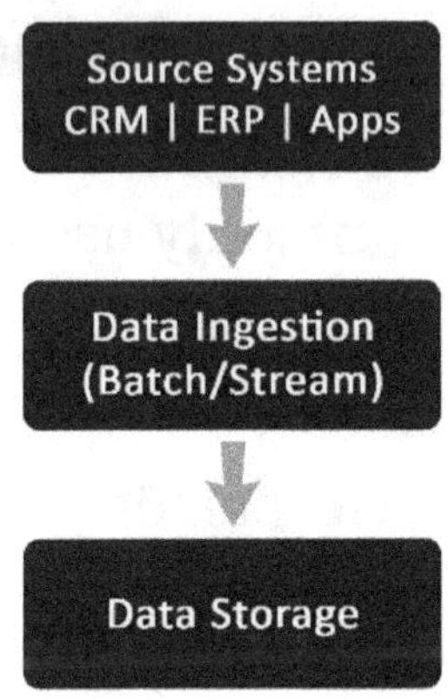

2.3 Data Storage Layers

Once data is collected, it must be stored in a system that allows efficient processing and retrieval. The storage layer is one of the most important components of a data architecture.

Different storage approaches exist depending on the type of data and the analytics requirements.

Data Warehouse Storage

Data warehouses store structured and curated data optimized for analytics and reporting. Data is typically transformed into well-defined schemas before being stored.

Advantages include:

- High query performance
- Strong data consistency
- Structured analytical models

Data Lake Storage

Data lakes store large volumes of raw data in their native format. This includes structured, semi-structured, and unstructured data.

Advantages include:

- Low-cost, scalable storage
- Flexibility for data exploration
- Support for advanced analytics and machine learning

Lakehouse Storage

The lake house architecture combines the strengths of both data lakes and data warehouses by enabling structured analytics directly on top of large-scale data lake storage.

This approach simplifies architecture by reducing the need for separate systems.

Storage Layer

The storage layer serves as the central repository where data is organized and prepared for analysis.

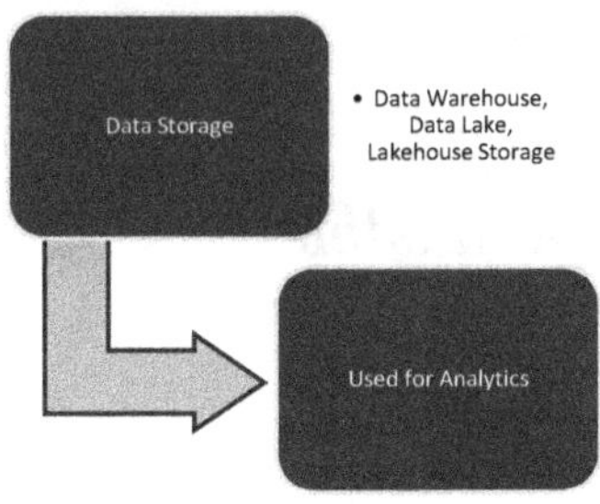

2.4 Data Processing and Transformation

Raw data is rarely ready for direct analysis. It often requires cleaning, transformation, and enrichment before it becomes useful for analytics or machine learning.

This step is handled by the data processing layer.

Data processing typically involves:

- Data cleaning and quality checks
- Data transformation and aggregation
- Schema standardization
- Joining datasets from multiple sources
- Feature engineering for machine learning

Processing can occur using several methods:

ETL (Extract, Transform, Load)

Data is transformed before being loaded into storage systems.

ELT (Extract, Load, Transform)

Data is first stored in raw form and transformed later during processing.

The ELT approach has become more popular in cloud-based data platforms because modern processing engines can handle transformations efficiently after the data is stored.

2.5 Data Serving and Consumption

After data is processed and prepared, it becomes available for consumption by various users and systems.

The data serving layer provides access to curated datasets and analytical outputs.

Common consumers of data include:

- Business intelligence dashboards
- Data analysts and scientists
- Machine learning models
- Operational applications

- External partners and APIs

The serving layer ensures that users can access data in a reliable, secure, and performance-optimized manner.

Data Consumption

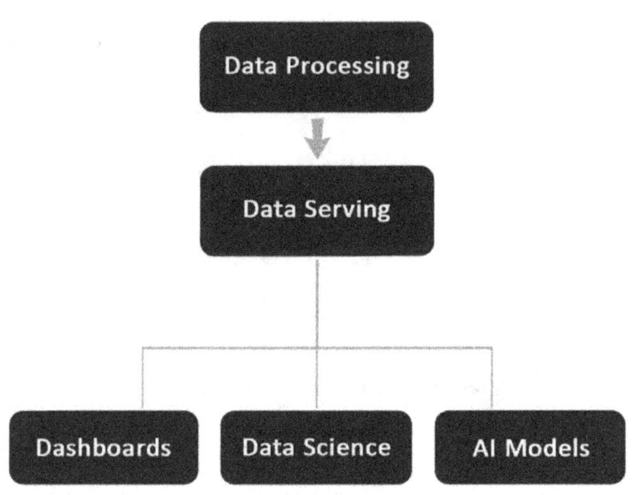

This stage transforms data into actionable insights and intelligent systems.

2.6 Data Governance and Security

As organizations become more data-driven, ensuring data reliability and security is increasingly critical.

Data governance defines the policies and processes that ensure data is trustworthy, compliant, and properly managed.

Key governance components include:

- Data quality management
- Access controls and permissions
- Data lineage tracking
- Regulatory compliance
- Privacy protection

Strong governance ensures that users can trust the data they rely on for decision-making.

Without governance, even the most sophisticated data architecture can fail because stakeholders lose confidence in the accuracy of the information.

2.7 Metadata Management and Data Catalogs

The final building block of modern data architecture is metadata management.

Metadata describes information about the data itself, such as:

- Data definitions
- Data ownership
- Data lineage
- Data usage patterns

Metadata systems help organizations understand where data comes from, how it is transformed, and how it is used across the enterprise.

Data catalogs build on metadata to create searchable inventories of datasets. These catalogs allow users to quickly discover relevant data and understand its context.

Metadata-driven architectures are becoming increasingly important because they enable automation, governance, and better collaboration across teams.

Bringing the Building Blocks Together

When combined, these building blocks form a complete data architecture.

Governance, Security and Metadata open across all layers

Although technologies may change over time, these foundational layers remain consistent across most modern data platforms.

By understanding these components, architects and engineers can design systems that are flexible, scalable, and aligned with business goals.

In the next chapter, we will explore the major data architecture paradigms that combine these building blocks into different architectural models, such as data warehouses, data lakes, lakehouses, data mesh, and data fabric.

Chapter 3: Understanding Modern Data Architecture Paradigms

As organizations increasingly rely on data for decision-making, analytics, and artificial intelligence, several architectural paradigms have emerged to address the challenges of storing, managing, and analyzing large volumes of data. While these architectures share common building blocks, they differ in how those components are organized and used. .

Understanding these paradigms is essential because organizations often struggle to determine which approach best fits their needs. In this chapter, we will explore five major architecture models used in modern data platforms: data warehouses, data lakes, lakehouses, data mesh, and data fabric. Each model addresses specific challenges and offers unique advantages.

3.1 Data Warehouse Architecture

The data warehouse is one of the earliest and most widely adopted data architecture paradigms. It was designed to support business intelligence and reporting by consolidating structured data from multiple operational systems into a centralized repository.

In a typical data warehouse architecture, data from transactional systems such as CRM, ERP, and financial

systems is extracted, transformed, and loaded into a centralized database optimized for analytical queries.

Key Characteristics

- Centralized storage for structured data
- Optimized for analytical queries
- Schema-based data modeling
- Strong data governance and consistency

Example Use Case

Consider a retail company that wants to analyze sales performance across different regions and product categories. The company collects data from:

- Point-of-sale systems
- Inventory management systems
- Customer relationship management platforms

A data warehouse consolidates this information and allows business leaders to generate reports such as:

- Monthly sales performance
- Top-performing products
- Regional revenue comparisons

Data Warehouse Architecture

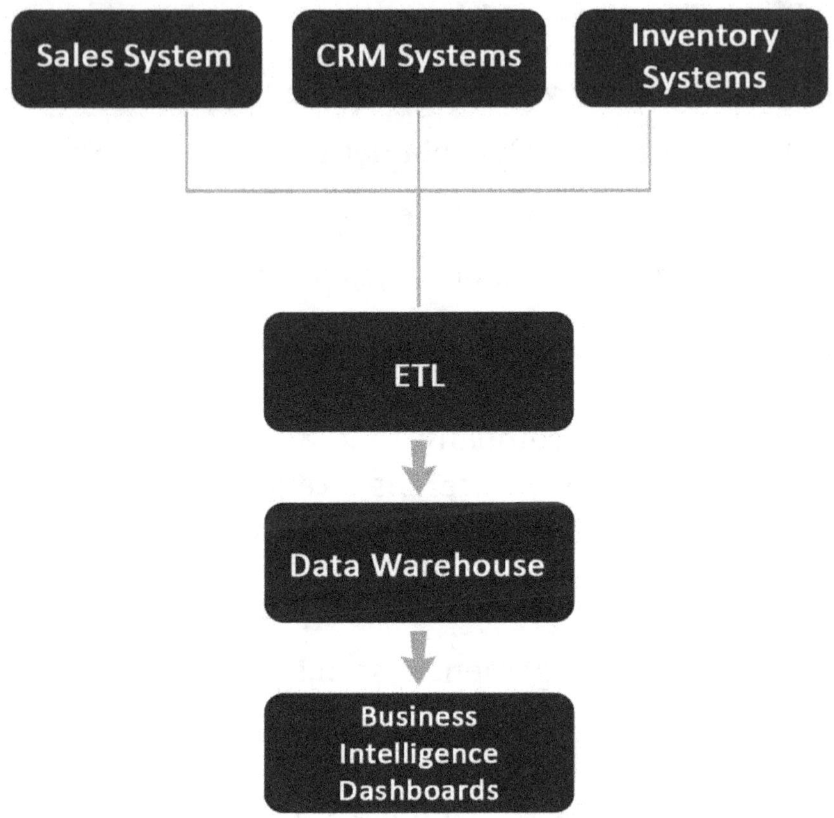

Although data warehouses provide reliable analytics environments, they struggle with large volumes of unstructured data, such as logs, images, and IoT data.

3.2 Data Lake Architecture

The data lake emerged to address the limitations of traditional data warehouses. Instead of storing only structured data, data lakes allow organizations to store large volumes of raw data in its original format.

This approach provides flexibility and scalability, making it suitable for big data analytics and machine learning workloads.

Key Characteristics

- Stores structured and unstructured data
- Highly scalable storage
- Schema-on-read approach
- Supports advanced analytics and data science

Example Use Case

A global e-commerce platform generates massive amounts of data every day, including:

- Website clickstream data
- Product browsing behavior
- Customer reviews
- Application logs

Instead of forcing all this data into structured schemas, the company stores it in a data lake. Data scientists then explore this data to build recommendation systems and predictive analytics models.

Data Lake Architecture

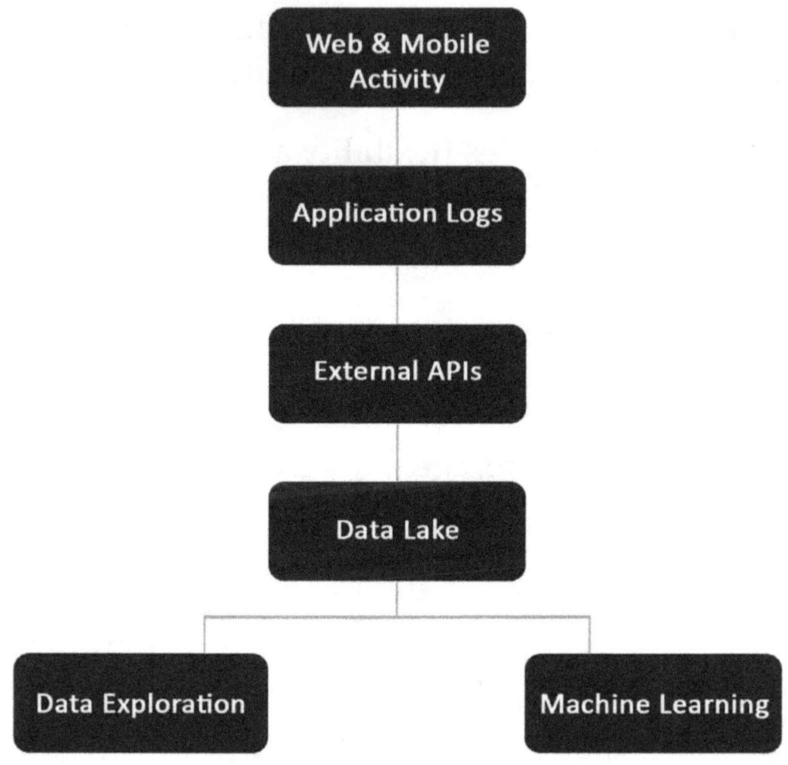

While data lakes enable large-scale storage, they can become disorganized if governance and metadata management are not properly implemented.

3.3 The Lakehouse Model

The lakehouse architecture was developed to combine the strengths of both data warehouses and data lakes. It allows organizations to store large volumes of data in a lake while also supporting structured analytics like a warehouse.

The lakehouse introduces features such as data reliability, transaction support, and schema enforcement on top of scalable storage.

Key Characteristics

- Unified storage for analytics and AI
- Combines warehouse performance with lake scalability
- Supports both structured and unstructured data
- Enables real-time analytics and machine learning

Example Use Case

A healthcare analytics company needs to process:

- Electronic health records
- Medical imaging data
- Clinical trial datasets
- Real-time patient monitoring streams

A lakehouse architecture enables the company to store all these datasets in a unified platform while supporting both reporting and AI-driven predictive analytics.

Lakehouse Architecture

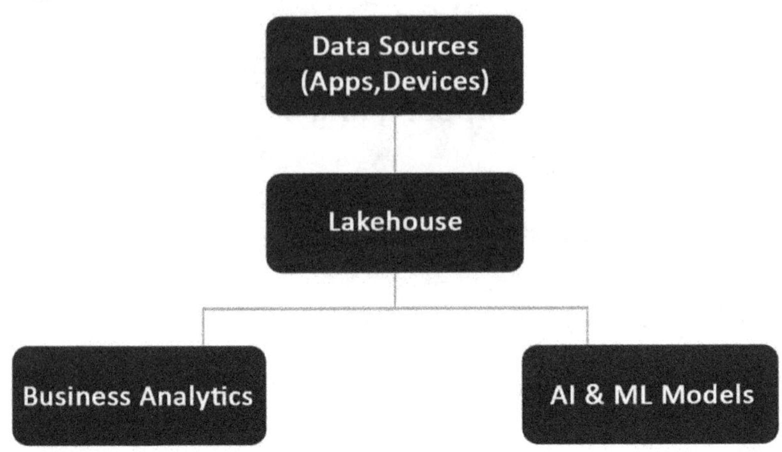

Lakehouse architectures are increasingly becoming the foundation for modern data platforms because they simplify infrastructure while supporting diverse workloads.

3.4 Data Mesh and Domain-Oriented Architecture

As organizations scale, centralized data teams often become bottlenecks. The data mesh architecture addresses this problem by decentralizing data ownership and treating data as a product owned by domain teams.

Instead of relying on a single central data platform team, different business domains manage their own data pipelines and datasets while following shared governance standards.

Key Characteristics

- Domain-based data ownership
- Data treated as a product
- Decentralized data management
- Federated governance

Example Use Case

Consider a large financial services organization with multiple business domains, such as:

- Retail banking
- Investment services
- Risk management
- Customer analytics

Each domain team manages its own datasets and publishes them as reusable data products for other teams to consume.

Pictorial Representation: Data Mesh

Data mesh improves scalability and domain expertise but requires strong governance frameworks to ensure consistency.

3.5 Data Fabric and Metadata-Driven Integration

The data fabric architecture focuses on creating a unified data layer across distributed systems using metadata and automation.

Instead of physically centralizing all data, data fabric connects different systems and enables users to access data regardless of where it resides.

Key Characteristics

- Metadata-driven integration
- Unified access to distributed data
- Automation and intelligent data management
- Supports hybrid and multi-cloud environments

Example Use Case

A global enterprise may have data stored across multiple platforms, such as:

- Cloud storage systems
- On-premises databases
- SaaS applications
- Partner systems

A data fabric architecture allows analysts and applications to access this data seamlessly without needing to move everything into a single repository.

Data Fabric

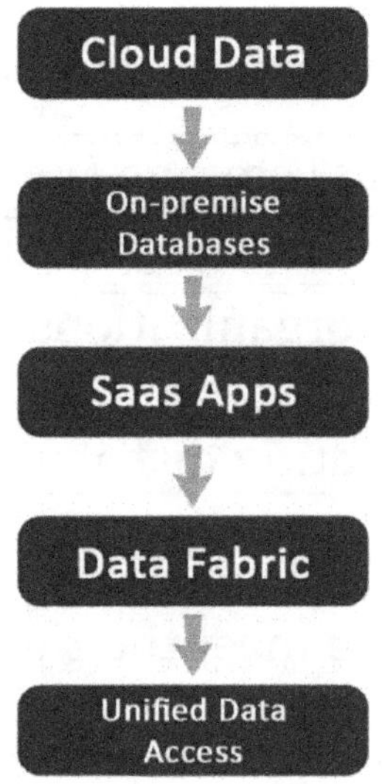

Data fabric architectures are particularly useful in organizations with complex data ecosystems and distributed infrastructure.

Comparing Architecture Paradigms

Each architecture paradigm addresses different challenges:

Architecture	Best Use Case
Data Warehouse	Structured analytics and reporting
Data Lake	Big data storage and exploration
Lakehouse	Unified analytics and AI workloads
Data Mesh	Large organizations with multiple data domains
Data Fabric	Integrating distributed data environments

In practice, many organizations combine elements of multiple architectures to meet their needs.

Understanding these paradigms helps architects make informed decisions about how to design scalable and future-ready data platforms.

In the next chapter, we will explore how organizations can choose the right architecture based on their data requirements, organizational structure, and analytics maturity.

Chapter 4: Choosing the Right Architecture for Your Organization

Selecting the right data architecture is one of the most important decisions an organization can make in its data journey. With numerous technologies and architectural paradigms available today, many organizations struggle to determine which approach best fits their needs. Often, teams adopt technologies based on trends, vendor recommendations, or isolated technical preferences rather than aligning architectural choices with real business requirements.

The truth is that there is no universal architecture that works for every organization. The right architecture depends on factors such as data volume, organizational structure, analytics maturity, regulatory requirements, and long-term strategic goals.

This chapter introduces a practical framework that organizations can use to evaluate their needs and choose the most suitable data architecture.

4.1 Understanding Business and Data Requirements

Before selecting any technology or architectural model, organizations must clearly understand their business objectives and data requirements.

Data architectures should always support business outcomes. A well-designed architecture enables organizations to answer critical questions, automate processes, and generate insights that drive decision-making.

Some important questions to consider include:

- What types of insights does the organization need?
- How quickly must data be available for analysis?
- What types of data are being generated?
- Who are the primary consumers of the data?

What level of reliability and governance is required?

For example, a retail organization focused on daily sales reporting may require a stable data warehouse environment. In contrast, a digital platform that relies on real-time user behavior analytics may need a streaming architecture combined with a scalable data lake.

Understanding these requirements helps organizations avoid over-engineering solutions or adopting technologies that add unnecessary complexity.

4.2 Data Volume, Variety, and Velocity Considerations

Another critical factor in architectural design is the nature of the data itself. Data systems must be capable of handling the scale and characteristics of the data being generated.

Three commonly used dimensions help evaluate data requirements:

Data Volume

This refers to the total amount of data generated and stored by the organization. Some organizations process gigabytes of data, while others handle petabytes.

Large-scale data environments often require distributed storage systems such as data lakes or lakehouse architectures.

Data Variety

Modern organizations generate multiple types of data, including:

- Structured data from transactional systems
- Semi-structured data, such as logs and JSON files
- Unstructured data, including images, audio, and documents

Architectures that support multiple data formats provide greater flexibility for analytics and machine learning use cases.

Data Velocity

Velocity refers to how quickly data is generated and needs to be processed. Some systems operate with daily batch updates, while others require real-time processing.

For example, fraud detection systems often require real-time data processing to identify suspicious transactions immediately.

Data Characteristics

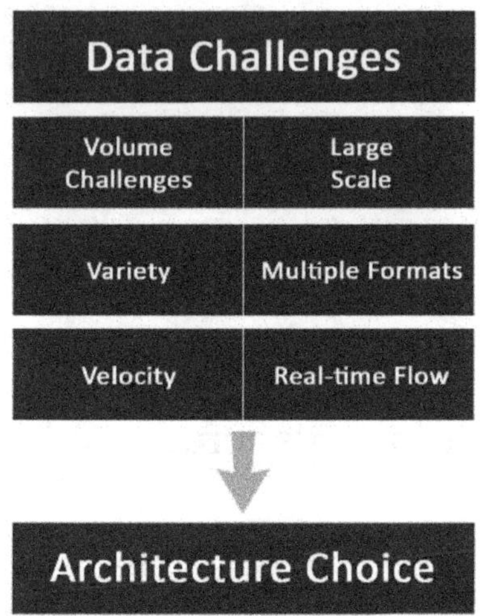

Organizations must evaluate these dimensions carefully to ensure that their architecture can handle current workloads while also scaling for future growth.

4.3 Organizational Structure and Data Ownership

The structure of an organization also plays a significant role in architectural design.

In smaller organizations, a centralized data team may manage all aspects of the data platform, including ingestion pipelines, data modeling, and analytics.

However, as organizations grow, data responsibilities often become distributed across multiple departments or business units. Each domain may generate its own datasets and analytics requirements.

In such cases, architectures that support domain ownership, such as data mesh, may provide advantages. Domain-oriented architectures allow teams to manage their own data products while maintaining shared governance standards.

For example, in a large enterprise:

- The marketing team may manage customer engagement data
- The finance team may manage revenue and cost data
- The operations team may manage supply chain data

Allowing these teams to own their datasets improves scalability and accountability while reducing bottlenecks in centralized teams.

4.4 Analytics and AI Maturity Levels

Another important consideration is the organization's analytics maturity.

Not every organization requires advanced machine learning or real-time analytics capabilities. Some organizations are still in the early stages of building basic reporting systems.

Understanding the maturity level of the organization helps determine the appropriate architecture.

Early Stage

Organizations at this stage typically focus on:

- Basic reporting
- Data consolidation
- Business intelligence dashboards

A well-structured data warehouse architecture may be sufficient for these needs.

Intermediate Stage

Organizations begin expanding analytics capabilities, including:

- Self-service analytics
- Data exploration
- Data science experimentation

A data lake or lakehouse architecture often supports these capabilities.

Advanced Stage

Highly mature organizations use data to power:

- Artificial intelligence systems
- Real-time decision engines

- Automated operational processes

These organizations often implement lakehouse, streaming, or domain-oriented architectures to support complex workloads.

Analytics Maturity

Matching architecture complexity with analytics maturity helps organizations evolve their data platforms gradually rather than attempting large-scale transformations all at once.

4.5 Governance and Compliance Requirements

Data governance and regulatory compliance are increasingly important considerations in architecture design.

Organizations operating in regulated industries such as healthcare, finance, and telecommunications must ensure that their data platforms support strict compliance standards.

Governance requirements often include:

- Data privacy protections
- Access control mechanisms
- Data lineage tracking
- Audit capabilities
- Regulatory reporting

Architectures that incorporate governance capabilities from the beginning are far more sustainable than those that attempt to add governance later.

For example, centralized data warehouses often provide strong governance controls, while distributed architectures require additional mechanisms to ensure compliance across domains.

4.6 Architecture Decision Framework

To simplify architecture selection, organizations can use a structured decision framework that evaluates several key dimensions.

Step 1: Assess Data Characteristics

- What is the scale of data?
- How many formats are involved?
- Is real-time processing required?

Step 2: Evaluate Business Needs

- What insights are required?
- Who are the data consumers?
- How frequently are reports needed?

Step 3: Evaluate Organizational Model

- Is data centralized or distributed across teams?
- Who owns the data products?

Step 4: Evaluate Governance Requirements

- Are there regulatory constraints?
- What level of security and auditing is required?

Step 5: Plan for Future Growth

- Will the organization adopt AI or advanced analytics?
- How quickly will data volumes grow?

Architecture Decision Flow

This framework allows organizations to approach architecture design methodically rather than relying on assumptions or technology trends.

Final Thoughts

Choosing the right data architecture is not simply a technical decision. It is a strategic one. The architecture must align with business goals, organizational structure, and future innovation plans.

Successful organizations recognize that data architectures should evolve gradually as requirements change. Instead of attempting to implement the most advanced architecture immediately, they build scalable foundations that can adapt over time.

In the next chapter, we will explore what a modern data platform blueprint looks like and how organizations design architectures that support both analytics and artificial intelligence at scale.

Chapter 5: The Modern Data Platform Blueprint

As organizations increasingly rely on data to drive decision-making, traditional data systems are often no longer sufficient. Modern businesses require platforms that can handle massive volumes of data, support advanced analytics, enable artificial intelligence, and deliver insights in near real time. This demand has led to the emergence of modern data platforms, flexible and scalable architectures designed to support the full lifecycle of data.

A modern data platform is not defined by a single tool or technology. Instead, it is a well-designed architecture that integrates multiple components to manage data efficiently from ingestion to consumption. In this chapter, we explore the key characteristics and architectural principles that define a modern data platform.

5.1 Characteristics of Modern Data Platforms

Modern data platforms are designed to overcome the limitations of earlier architectures while supporting a broader range of analytics workloads. Several key characteristics distinguish modern platforms from traditional systems.

Scalability

Modern platforms must scale to accommodate growing volumes of data. As organizations generate more data through digital applications, IoT devices, and user interactions, the platform must expand without a major redesign.

Scalable platforms allow organizations to process and analyze large datasets without performance bottlenecks.

Flexibility

A modern platform must support multiple data types, including structured, semi-structured, and unstructured data. Flexibility allows organizations to ingest data from diverse sources such as APIs, logs, streaming events, and enterprise systems.

Support for Advanced Analytics

Modern organizations increasingly rely on machine learning and artificial intelligence. Data platforms must therefore support data science workflows, experimentation environments, and model deployment pipelines.

Reliability and Governance

Trust in data is essential. Modern platforms integrate governance capabilities such as data quality monitoring, lineage tracking, and access control mechanisms.

These characteristics ensure that the data platform becomes a reliable foundation for analytics and decision-making.

5.2 Cloud-Native Architecture Patterns

One of the most significant shifts in data architecture has been the adoption of cloud-native architectures.

Cloud platforms allow organizations to store and process large volumes of data without managing physical infrastructure. Instead of purchasing hardware and maintaining servers, teams can access scalable storage and compute resources on demand.

Cloud-native data platforms offer several advantages:

- Elastic scalability
- Reduced infrastructure management
- Faster deployment of analytics environments
- Integration with a wide range of data services

Another important concept in cloud architectures is the separation of storage and compute. In traditional systems, storage and processing resources were tightly coupled. Modern architectures separate these components so that each can scale independently.

Cloud Data Platform

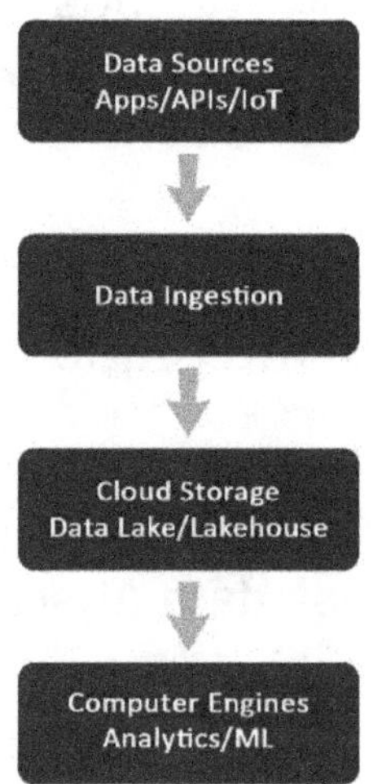

This architecture allows organizations to scale storage and processing independently, making it easier to support diverse analytics workloads.

5.3 Batch and Real-Time Data Integration

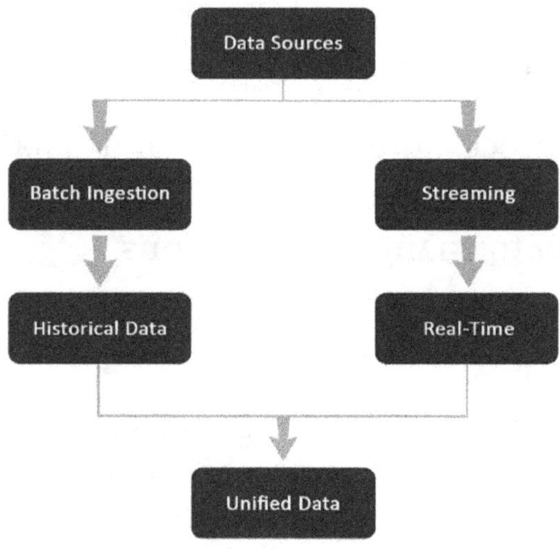

Modern organizations require insights at different speeds. Some analytics workloads rely on historical data updated periodically, while others require real-time data streams.

A modern data platform must therefore support both batch and real-time data integration.

Batch Processing

Batch pipelines process data at scheduled intervals. They are commonly used for tasks such as:

- Financial reporting
- Daily sales aggregation
- Data warehouse updates

Batch processing remains essential because it allows organizations to process large volumes of historical data efficiently.

Real-Time Processing

Real-time processing captures and analyzes data as events occur. This capability enables organizations to respond quickly to changing conditions.

Examples of real-time use cases include:

- Fraud detection in banking transactions
- Monitoring system performance
- Personalized recommendations on digital platforms

Modern architectures integrate both processing models to support different business needs.

Batch and Real-Time Processing

Combining these approaches ensures that organizations can analyze both historical trends and live operational data.

5.4 Unified Data Storage and Analytics

Modern architectures aim to reduce complexity by unifying storage and analytics environments. Instead of maintaining separate systems for data lakes and warehouses, many organizations adopt lakehouse architectures that combine the strengths of both approaches.

A unified platform allows organizations to:

- Store large volumes of raw data
- Run high-performance analytical queries
- Support machine learning workloads
- Maintain governance and data reliability

This approach simplifies architecture by reducing data duplication and eliminating the need for multiple data movement pipelines.

Unified platforms also make it easier for different teams, such as data engineers, analysts, and data scientists, to collaborate on the same datasets.

Pictorial Representation: Unified Data Platform

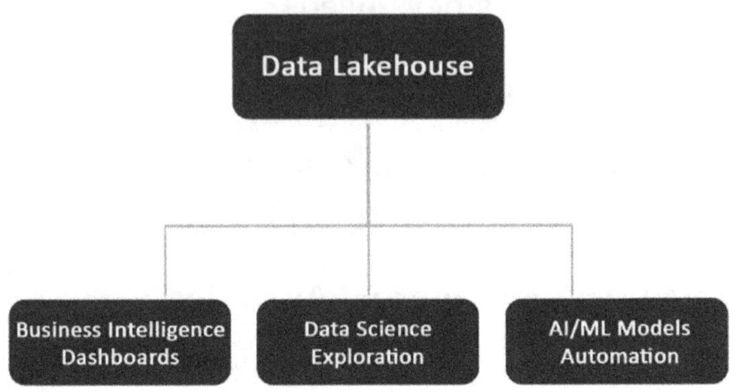

By enabling multiple workloads on a shared platform, organizations can reduce operational complexity and improve collaboration across teams.

5.5 Metadata-Driven Architecture

As data platforms grow, managing datasets becomes increasingly challenging. Organizations may store thousands of tables and datasets across multiple systems.

To manage this complexity, modern data architectures rely heavily on metadata.

Metadata provides information about data, including:

- Data definitions
- Data lineage
- Data ownership
- Data quality metrics
- Access permissions

Metadata systems enable the creation of data catalogs, which help users discover and understand available datasets.

Metadata-driven architectures also support automation. For example, governance policies can automatically enforce security rules based on metadata attributes.

This approach improves transparency and ensures that data remains trustworthy across the organization.

5.6 Scalability and Performance Considerations

Designing a modern data platform also requires careful attention to performance and scalability. As organizations grow, the platform must handle increasing data volumes and user demand without degradation.

Several architectural practices help achieve this goal:

Distributed Processing

Distributed computing frameworks divide large workloads across multiple processing nodes, allowing systems to analyze large datasets quickly.

Data Partitioning

Partitioning divides large datasets into smaller segments based on logical criteria such as time or geography. This improves query performance by limiting the amount of data that needs to be scanned.

Caching and Optimization

Caching frequently accessed data reduces query latency and improves user experience for dashboards and analytics tools.

Elastic Resource Allocation

Cloud platforms allow compute resources to scale automatically based on workload demands, ensuring consistent performance even during peak usage.

Pictorial Representation: Scalable Architecture

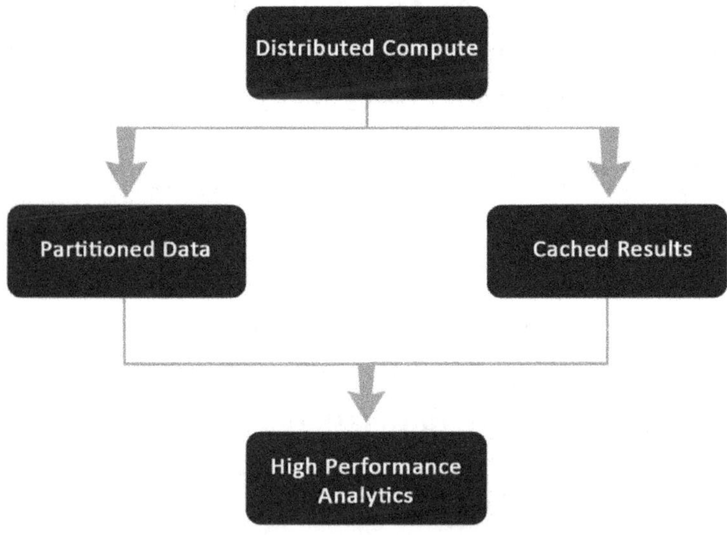

These techniques ensure that modern data platforms remain responsive and efficient even as data volumes grow.

Final Thoughts

A modern data platform serves as the foundation for analytics, decision-making, and artificial intelligence within an organization. By integrating scalable storage, flexible processing frameworks, real-time data pipelines, and strong governance capabilities, modern architectures enable organizations to unlock the full value of their data.

However, building such platforms also introduces new challenges. As architectures become more sophisticated, organizations must carefully manage complexity to avoid fragmented systems and inefficient pipelines.

In the next chapter, we will explore how organizations can eliminate data silos and pipeline complexity, ensuring that their data platforms remain manageable, reliable, and scalable as they evolve.

Chapter 6: Eliminating Data Silos and Pipeline Complexity

As organizations expand their data initiatives, one of the most common challenges they encounter is the proliferation of data silos and complex data pipelines. Despite investing heavily in modern data platforms and advanced analytics tools, many organizations still struggle with fragmented datasets, duplicated pipelines, and inconsistent metrics.

Data silos occur when different teams or systems maintain isolated datasets that are not easily accessible or integrated with the broader data ecosystem. Pipeline complexity arises when multiple data workflows are built independently without standardization or shared governance.

These issues reduce the effectiveness of data platforms and create barriers to analytics and artificial intelligence initiatives. This chapter explores the root causes of data silos and pipeline complexity and presents architectural strategies for building unified, scalable data systems.

6.1 The Problem of Fragmented Data Systems

Data silos typically emerge when organizations grow rapidly or adopt new technologies without establishing a consistent data architecture strategy. Different departments often implement their own data solutions to meet immediate business needs.

For example:

- The marketing team may store customer engagement data in a marketing automation platform
- The sales team may maintain customer information in a CRM system
- The finance team may manage revenue and financial data in enterprise accounting systems

Although each system serves a specific purpose, the lack of integration between them creates fragmented datasets. As a result, analysts often spend more time locating and preparing data than performing meaningful analysis.

Fragmentation also creates challenges, such as:

- Conflicting business metrics
- Duplicate data pipelines
- Difficulty sharing insights across teams
- Increased operational costs

Without a unified architecture, organizations risk creating environments where data exists but is difficult to use effectively.

Pictorial Representation: Fragmented Data Silos

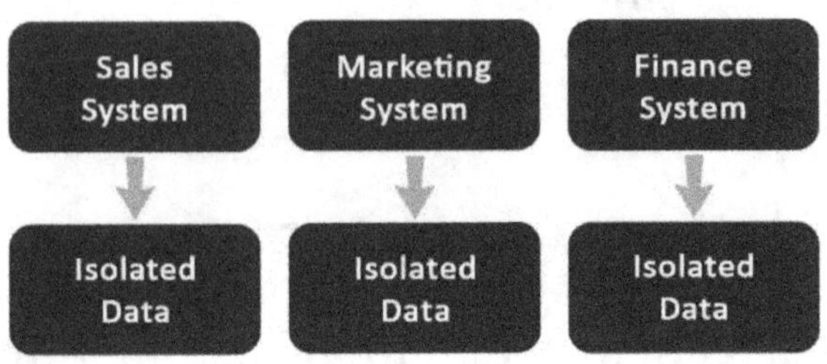

In this environment, each department operates independently, limiting the ability to generate unified insights.

6.2 Managing Data Pipelines Effectively

Data pipelines are responsible for moving and transforming data from source systems to analytics environments. As organizations expand their data operations, the number of pipelines often grows rapidly.

Without proper design principles, pipeline ecosystems can become difficult to maintain.

Common problems include:

- Duplicate data ingestion pipelines
- Inconsistent transformation logic
- Lack of monitoring and error handling
- Difficult debugging processes

For example, multiple teams may independently build pipelines that extract similar data from the same source system. This duplication increases infrastructure costs and introduces inconsistencies in data processing.

To address this challenge, organizations should adopt standardized pipeline frameworks that promote reusability and consistency.

Key practices include:

- Modular pipeline design
- Centralized orchestration tools
- Automated monitoring and alerts
- Version control for data transformations

Standardization ensures that pipelines remain manageable as the data ecosystem grows.

Pictorial Representation: Pipeline Complexity

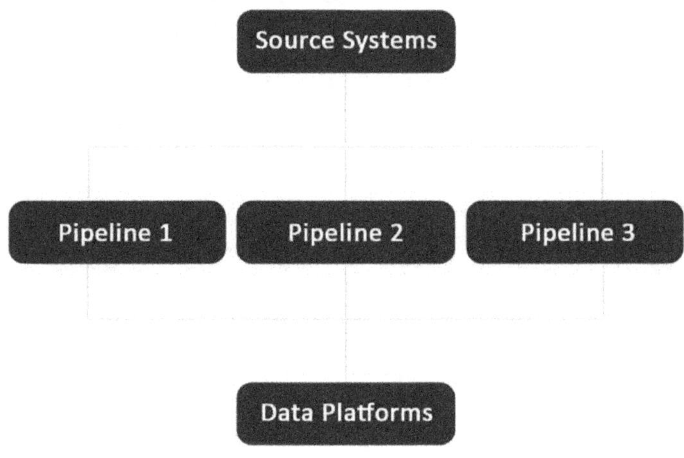

Without coordination, pipelines can multiply quickly and create unnecessary complexity.

One of the most effective ways to reduce pipeline complexity is to create reusable data assets.

Reusable assets include:

- Standardized data ingestion pipelines
- Shared transformation logic
- Curated datasets
- Common data models

Instead of building separate pipelines for each analytics use case, organizations can develop shared datasets that multiple teams can use.

For example, a customer data model can consolidate information from CRM systems, transaction databases, and digital engagement platforms. Once this dataset is created and governed, multiple teams, such as marketing, sales, and product development, can use it for analytics.

Reusable assets improve efficiency and ensure consistency across analytics workloads.

Pictorial Representation: Reusable Data Assets

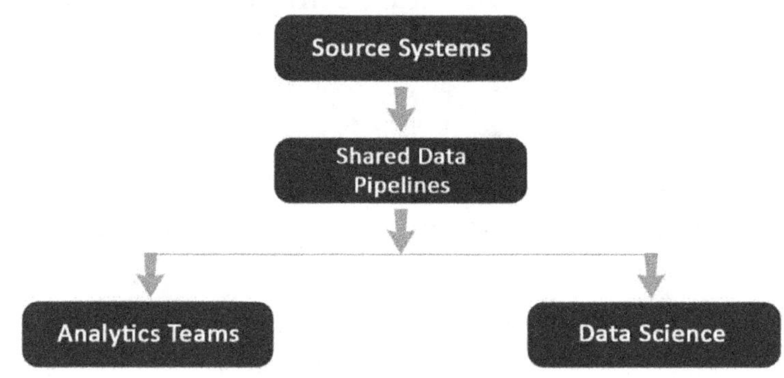

By sharing common pipelines and datasets, organizations reduce duplication and streamline data workflows.

6.4 Establishing a Unified Data View

A unified data architecture allows organizations to consolidate datasets and provide consistent access across departments.

This often involves creating curated data layers that standardize key business entities such as customers, products, transactions, and operations.

The benefits of unified data views include:

- Consistent business definitions
- Improved collaboration across teams
- Faster analytics development
- Reliable data for decision-making

For example, a unified customer 360 dataset may integrate information from marketing campaigns, customer service interactions, transaction history, and website activity.

This unified view allows organizations to better understand customer behavior and personalize services.

Pictorial Representation: Unified Data View

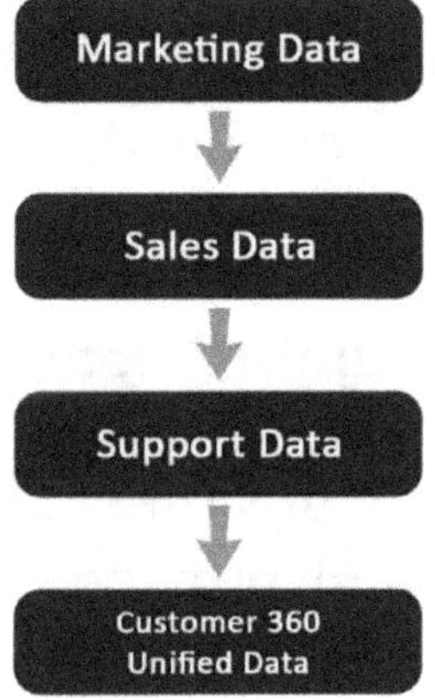

This integrated dataset becomes a reliable foundation for analytics and business insights.

6.5 The Role of Data Products

An emerging concept in modern data architecture is the idea of data products.

A data product treats data as a reusable asset designed for consumption by other teams or systems. Instead of simply storing data, organizations design datasets that are well documented, reliable, and easily accessible.

A typical data product includes:

- A curated dataset
- Documentation and metadata
- Defined data owners
- Quality monitoring processes
- Clear usage guidelines

Data products help organizations scale data platforms by enabling teams to share reliable datasets without relying on centralized data teams for every request.

AI Fundamentals and the Importance of Data Architecture

Artificial intelligence systems depend heavily on high-quality data pipelines and integrated datasets. Without a reliable data architecture, AI initiatives often fail due to inconsistent or incomplete data.

Several fundamental AI concepts highlight the importance of strong data architecture.

Training Data

Machine learning models learn patterns from historical data known as training data. If training data is fragmented or inconsistent, model performance suffers.

Feature Engineering

Feature engineering involves transforming raw data into meaningful variables that improve model predictions. This process requires well-structured data pipelines and standardized datasets.

Model Deployment

Once models are trained, they must be integrated into operational systems. This often requires real-time data pipelines that deliver fresh data to prediction systems.

Pictorial Representation: Data Architecture for AI

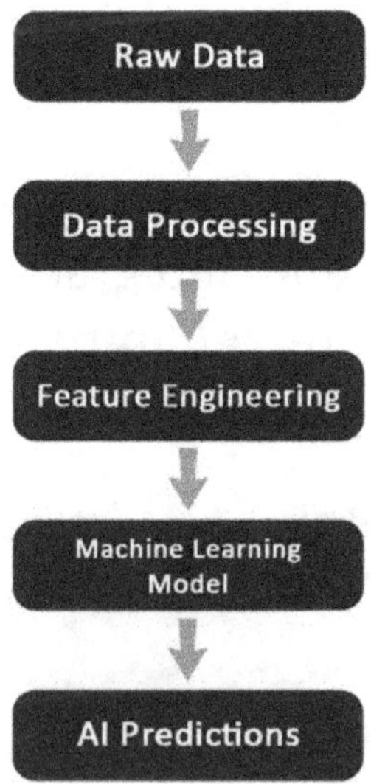

This flow illustrates how modern data architectures provide the foundation for AI-driven systems.

Final Thoughts

Eliminating data silos and pipeline complexity is essential for organizations seeking to unlock the full value of their data. Fragmented systems and duplicated pipelines not only increase operational costs but also slow innovation and reduce trust in data.

By adopting shared pipelines, reusable data assets, unified data models, and well-defined data products, organizations can simplify their data ecosystems and improve collaboration across teams.

At the same time, modern architectures must support emerging technologies such as artificial intelligence and machine learning. These systems rely heavily on reliable data pipelines, high-quality datasets, and scalable infrastructure.

In the next chapter, we will explore how organizations can design AI-ready data architectures, enabling advanced analytics, intelligent systems, and automated decision-making.

Chapter 7: Designing AI-Ready Data Architectures

Artificial intelligence (AI) is rapidly transforming how organizations operate, make decisions, and deliver value to customers. From predictive analytics and recommendation systems to intelligent automation and conversational interfaces, AI has become a strategic capability across industries. However, many AI initiatives fail to deliver meaningful results, not because of limitations in algorithms, but because of poor data architecture.

AI systems depend heavily on reliable, well-structured, and continuously updated data. Without strong data foundations, machine learning models cannot learn effectively, predictions become unreliable, and operational deployment becomes difficult. As a result, organizations seeking to leverage AI must first design AI-ready data architectures that support the entire lifecycle of data and models.

This chapter explores how modern data architectures enable artificial intelligence by supporting high-quality data pipelines, scalable processing environments, and integrated machine learning workflows.

7.1 Why AI Projects Depend on Data Architecture

Artificial intelligence systems rely on large volumes of data to identify patterns, make predictions, and automate decisions. Unlike traditional analytics systems, which often focus on historical reporting, AI models continuously learn from data and require ongoing updates.

Several challenges make data architecture critical for AI initiatives.

First, AI models require large datasets to achieve meaningful accuracy. These datasets often come from multiple systems, including operational databases, sensors, logs, and user interactions. Integrating these sources into a unified data platform is essential.

Second, AI models must be retrained regularly as new data becomes available. This requires automated data pipelines capable of continuously updating training datasets.

Third, AI systems often operate in real time, especially when powering recommendation engines, fraud detection systems, or intelligent assistants. Real-time data architectures are therefore necessary for delivering timely predictions.

Without a scalable and well-governed data architecture, organizations struggle to maintain reliable machine learning systems.

7.2 Data Quality and Data Readiness for AI

One of the most important factors influencing AI performance is data quality. Machine learning models are highly sensitive to inconsistencies, errors, and biases in training data.

If training data is incomplete, inaccurate, or inconsistent, the resulting model may produce unreliable predictions. This concept is often summarized by the phrase "garbage in, garbage out."

AI-ready architectures must therefore include mechanisms to ensure data quality throughout the data pipeline.

Key elements of data readiness include:

Data Cleaning

Data cleaning involves identifying and correcting errors such as missing values, duplicate records, and incorrect data formats.

Data Standardization

Data collected from different systems may use inconsistent formats or naming conventions. Standardizing these attributes ensures that datasets can be combined effectively.

Data Validation

Validation rules help ensure that incoming data meets predefined quality standards. These rules may check for anomalies, unexpected values, or incomplete records.

Pictorial Representation: Data Quality Pipeline

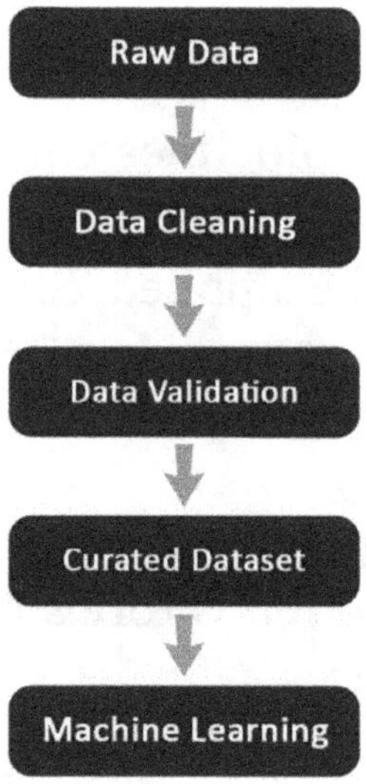

This pipeline ensures that AI models receive high-quality data inputs.

7.3 Feature Engineering and Data Pipelines

A central concept in machine learning is feature engineering. Features are the variables used by models to make predictions.

For example, a fraud detection model may use features such as:

- Transaction amount
- Transaction location
- Customer spending patterns
- Device type used for payment

These features are often derived from raw data using transformations, aggregations, and calculations.

Feature engineering pipelines convert raw datasets into structured features that improve model accuracy. Because these pipelines must be applied consistently during both training and prediction, they are often managed as part of the data architecture.

Organizations frequently implement feature stores, which act as centralized repositories for storing and sharing machine learning features.

Feature stores provide several benefits:

- Consistent feature definitions
- Reusable data transformations

- Reduced duplication across data science teams
- Improved model reproducibility

Feature Engineering Workflow

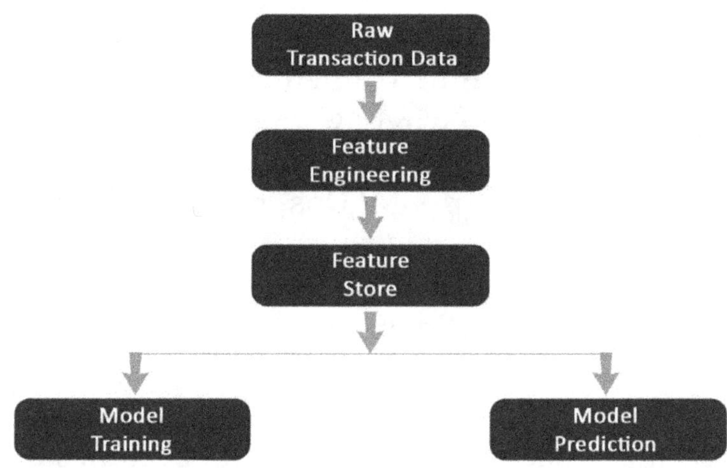

By standardizing features, organizations ensure that machine learning models use consistent data inputs across environments.

7.4 Integrating MLOps into Data Platforms

As AI systems become more complex, organizations must manage not only data pipelines but also machine learning pipelines. This discipline is commonly known as MLOps (Machine Learning Operations).

MLOps extends the principles of DevOps to machine learning systems by automating processes such as:

- Model training

- Model validation
- Model deployment
- Model monitoring

An AI-ready data architecture integrates MLOps capabilities directly into the data platform. This integration ensures that models can be trained and deployed using the same data infrastructure used for analytics.

Key components of MLOps-enabled architectures include:

Automated Training Pipelines

Data pipelines automatically prepare datasets and trigger model training processes when new data becomes available.

Model Versioning

Each version of a machine learning model is tracked and stored, enabling teams to compare performance and revert to previous versions if necessary.

Model Monitoring

Once deployed, models must be monitored to ensure that predictions remain accurate as data patterns change.

MLOps Architecture

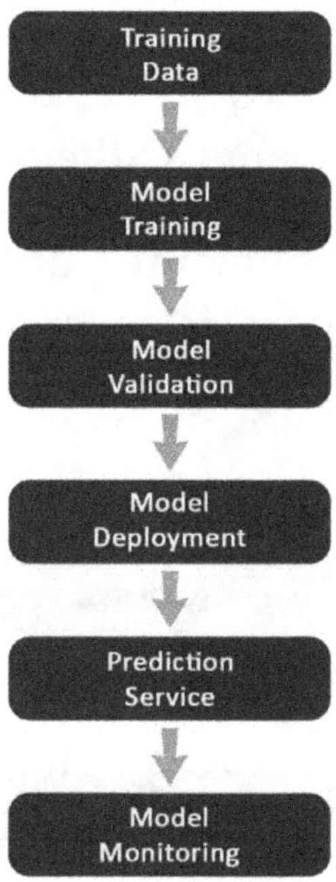

This automated workflow ensures that machine learning systems remain reliable over time.

7.5 Real-Time Data for Intelligent Systems

Many modern AI systems rely on real-time data processing. These systems must analyze incoming events immediately to generate predictions or trigger automated actions.

Examples of real-time AI applications include:

- Fraud detection in financial transactions
- Personalized product recommendations

- Predictive maintenance in manufacturing
- Intelligent traffic management systems

Real-time architectures often rely on streaming data pipelines that process events as they occur.

In a streaming architecture, data flows continuously through a pipeline where it is processed, enriched, and delivered to machine learning models.

Real-Time AI Architecture

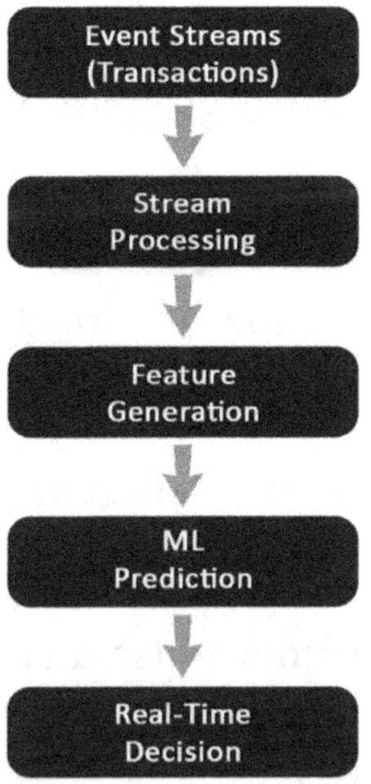

This architecture allows organizations to respond to events instantly, enabling intelligent automation and proactive decision-making.

Final Thoughts

Artificial intelligence represents one of the most transformative capabilities available to modern organizations. However, successful AI adoption depends heavily on the strength of the underlying data architecture.

AI-ready architectures must support high-quality data pipelines, standardized feature engineering processes, scalable machine learning environments, and automated MLOps workflows. They must also enable both batch and real-time data processing to support diverse AI use cases.

Organizations that invest in these architectural foundations are better positioned to build intelligent systems that generate reliable insights and automate complex decisions.

In the next chapter, we will explore real-world data architecture patterns that organizations use to implement these concepts in practical, scalable data platforms.

Chapter 8: Real-World Data Architecture Patterns

Throughout this book, we have explored the evolution of data architectures, the building blocks of modern data platforms, and the role of data in enabling analytics and artificial intelligence. However, understanding theory alone is not enough. Organizations must translate architectural principles into real-world architecture patterns that support practical business use cases.

A data architecture pattern represents a reusable blueprint that organizations can adopt when designing systems for analytics, real-time processing, or machine learning. These patterns guide how different components, such as data sources, pipelines, storage systems, and compute engines, work together to deliver insights and intelligence.

This chapter explores several commonly used data architecture patterns that organizations implement in modern data platforms.

8.1 Analytics Platform Architecture

One of the most widely used patterns in data architecture is the analytics platform architecture. This architecture is designed to support reporting, business intelligence, and advanced analytics across an organization.

In this architecture, data from multiple operational systems is collected and integrated into a centralized platform where it can be transformed and analyzed.

Typical data sources include:

- Transactional databases
- Enterprise applications
- Customer relationship management systems
- Website and application logs
- Third-party datasets

Data pipelines extract information from these sources and load it into a centralized storage layer, such as a data warehouse or data lake house. From there, analytics tools and dashboards can access curated datasets to generate insights.

This architecture allows organizations to build consistent business metrics and standardized reporting frameworks.

Example: Retail Business Analytics

Consider a retail organization that operates both physical stores and an online shopping platform. The company collects data from several systems:

- Point-of-sale systems in retail stores
- Online e-commerce transactions
- Inventory management systems
- Customer loyalty programs

By integrating these datasets into a centralized analytics platform, the company can answer important business questions such as:

- Which products sell best in different regions?
- How do online and in-store purchases compare?
- What customer segments generate the highest revenue?

Analytics Architecture

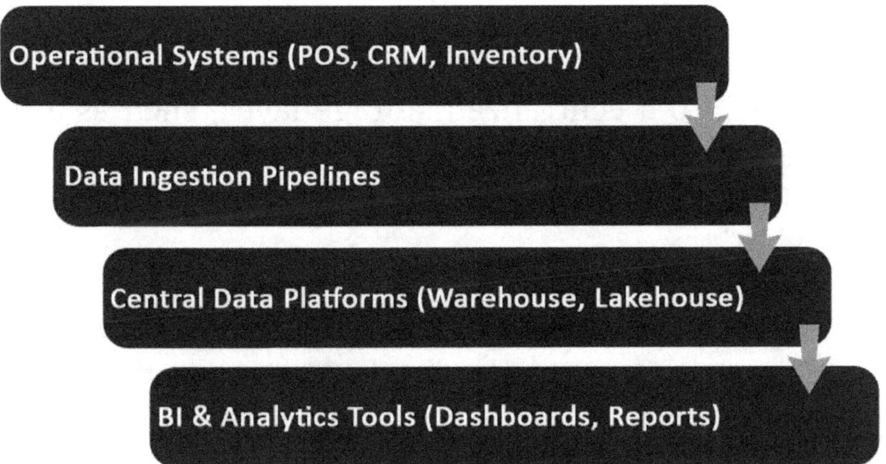

This architecture provides a unified view of business data for decision-makers.

8.2 Real-Time Streaming Architecture

In many industries, organizations cannot wait for daily or hourly reports. They must react to events as they occur.

This need has led to the adoption of real-time streaming architectures.

Streaming architectures process data continuously as it is generated. Instead of storing data first and analyzing it later, these systems analyze events immediately as they arrive.

Streaming data sources often include:

- IoT sensors
- Financial transactions
- Application logs
- User activity events
- Social media feeds

Real-time architectures rely on event streaming platforms and stream processing engines that analyze incoming data streams.

Example: Fraud Detection in Banking

Financial institutions must detect fraudulent transactions as quickly as possible. Waiting hours to analyze transactions could lead to significant financial losses.

A bank may implement a streaming architecture where every transaction is immediately analyzed by a fraud detection model.

The system performs the following steps:

1. A customer initiates a credit card transaction.

2. The transaction event is streamed into the data platform.
3. A machine learning model evaluates the transaction in real time.
4. If the model detects suspicious behavior, the transaction is flagged or blocked.

Streaming Data Architecture

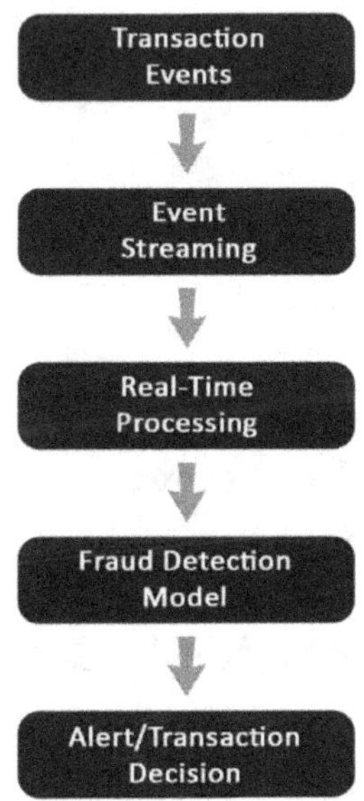

This architecture enables organizations to respond instantly to critical events.

8.3 AI and Machine Learning Platform Architecture

As organizations increasingly adopt artificial intelligence, they require architectures specifically designed to support machine learning workflows.

An AI platform architecture integrates data pipelines, model training environments, and deployment systems.

This architecture supports the complete lifecycle of machine learning:

- Data collection
- Data preparation
- Feature engineering
- Model training
- Model deployment
- Prediction services

Unlike traditional analytics platforms, AI architectures must support iterative experimentation. Data scientists frequently train multiple models, compare results, and refine algorithms.

Therefore, AI platforms must provide scalable compute environments capable of handling large datasets and complex training processes.

Example: Healthcare Predictive Analytics

A healthcare organization may use machine learning to predict patient readmission risk.

The system uses historical patient records, such as:

- Medical history
- Laboratory test results
- Treatment plans

- Hospital stay durations

A machine learning model analyzes these variables to predict whether a patient is likely to be readmitted within 30 days of discharge.

If the model predicts a high risk of readmission, healthcare providers can intervene earlier and improve patient outcomes.

AI Platform Architecture

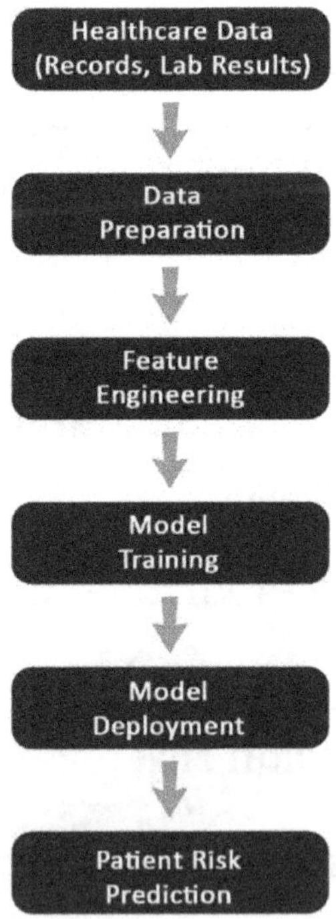

This architecture supports predictive analytics that improve healthcare decision-making.

8.4 Domain-Oriented Data Architecture

As organizations scale their data ecosystems, centralized data teams often become overwhelmed with requests from multiple departments. To address this challenge, some organizations adopt domain-oriented data architectures.

In this model, data ownership is distributed across business domains such as:

- Finance
- Marketing
- Operations
- Supply chain
- Customer experience

Each domain is responsible for managing and publishing its own data products. These data products are well-documented datasets that other teams can consume.

This approach improves scalability by allowing teams closest to the data to manage its quality and structure.

Example: E-Commerce Data Domains

An e-commerce organization may divide its data ecosystem into several domains:

- Customer domain, manages customer profiles and behavior data
- Product domain, maintains product catalog information

- Order domain, handles transaction and order fulfillment data
- Marketing domain, manages campaign performance data

Each domain team publishes curated datasets for use by other teams in analytics and AI.

Domain-Oriented Architecture

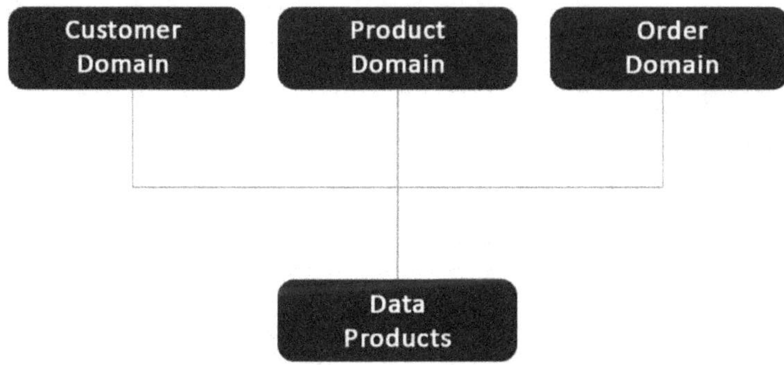

This architecture promotes decentralized data ownership while maintaining shared infrastructure.

Final Thoughts

Modern organizations operate in increasingly complex data environments. As data volumes grow and analytics use cases expand, designing scalable and flexible architectures becomes critical.

The architecture patterns explored in this chapter, analytics platforms, real-time streaming systems, AI platforms, and domain-oriented architectures, represent some of the most common approaches used by organizations today.

Each pattern addresses specific business needs:

- Analytics architectures support reporting and business intelligence
- Streaming architectures enable real-time decision-making
- AI platforms power predictive analytics and intelligent automation
- Domain-oriented architectures improve scalability through distributed data ownership

In practice, most organizations combine multiple architectural patterns within a single data platform. By understanding these patterns and applying them strategically, architects and data leaders can build systems that not only manage data efficiently but also unlock its full potential for innovation and competitive advantage.

With this foundation, readers are now equipped to understand modern data architectures and design platforms that support analytics, artificial intelligence, and future data-driven innovation.

Conclusion

The Future of Data Architecture

Every modern organization is becoming a data organization, whether it realizes it or not. Customer interactions, digital platforms, connected devices, and intelligent systems continuously generate enormous volumes of data. Within that data lies insight, innovation, and competitive advantage. But raw data alone does not create value. Architecture does.

Throughout this book, we explored how data architectures have evolved, from traditional data warehouses to modern cloud-native platforms, streaming systems, and AI-ready infrastructures. We examined the building blocks of modern data platforms, the challenges of fragmented pipelines and data silos, and the architectural patterns that organizations use to support analytics and artificial intelligence.

One important lesson emerges from all these discussions:

Successful data initiatives are rarely limited by technology. They are limited by architecture.

Many organizations invest in powerful tools, advanced analytics platforms, and cutting-edge AI models, yet struggle to realize their full potential. The underlying reason is often a lack of architectural clarity. Without a well-designed architecture, data becomes scattered, pipelines multiply uncontrollably, governance becomes difficult, and AI systems fail to scale.

A strong data architecture acts as the foundation that connects everything:

- Data sources
- Data pipelines
- Analytics platforms
- Machine learning systems
- Business decision-making

When architecture is designed thoughtfully, organizations can move faster, experiment more confidently, and unlock insights that were previously hidden.

But perhaps the most exciting aspect of data architecture is that it is still evolving. New paradigms such as lakehouse architectures, data mesh, AI-driven data platforms, and intelligent automation are reshaping how organizations manage and utilize information. The architects of tomorrow will not simply design systems that store data. They will design platforms that power intelligence itself.

For readers stepping into this world, the opportunity is enormous. Data architects today sit at the intersection of technology, strategy, and innovation. Their decisions influence how organizations understand customers, optimize operations, and build intelligent products.

In many ways, data architecture is like city planning. A city built without structure becomes chaotic and inefficient. Roads intersect randomly, resources are difficult to access, and growth becomes unsustainable. But when a city is designed with thoughtful planning, it becomes a thriving ecosystem where people, ideas, and opportunities flow freely.

The same is true for data.

When data architecture is designed with vision and discipline, organizations create ecosystems where information flows seamlessly, insights emerge naturally, and innovation accelerates.

And that is the real purpose of deciphering data architectures: not simply to understand technology, but to design the invisible infrastructure that powers the intelligent organizations of the future.

This Is Fact

Technology will continue to change. Tools will evolve. New platforms will appear. But the need for clear, scalable, and intelligent data architecture will only grow. The next breakthrough product, life-saving healthcare model, or transformative business insight may not begin with an algorithm. It may begin with a well-designed data architecture.

www.ingramcontent.com/pod-product-compliance
Lightning Source LLC
La Vergne TN
LVHW010615110826
845149LV00003B/920

* 9 7 8 1 9 7 2 0 0 4 4 2 5 *